5 Steps to
Counteract Stress

Learn about

5 Steps to Counteract Stress

Dr. ANJALI ARORA

STERLING PAPERBACKS
An imprint of
Sterling Publishers (P) Ltd.
Regd. Office: A1/256 Safdarjung Enclave,
New Delhi-110029. CIN: U22110DL1964PTC211907
Tel: 26387070, 26386209; Fax: 91-11-26383788
E-mail: mail@sterlingpublishers.com
www.sterlingpublishers.com

5 Steps to
Counteract Stress
© 2017, *Dr. Anjali Arora*
arora_doc@hotmail.com
ISBN 978 81 207 3245 2
Reprint 2018

The author wishes to thank all academicians, scientists and writers who have been a source of inspiration.

The author and publisher specifically disclaim any liability, loss or risk, whatsoever, personal or otherwise, which is incurred as a consequence, directly or indirectly of the use and application of any of the contents of this book.

All rights are reserved.
No part of this publication may be reproduced, stored in a retrieval system or transmitted, in any form or by any means, mechanical, photocopying, recording or otherwise, without prior written permission of the authors.

Printed and Published in India by

Sterling Publishers Pvt. Ltd.,
Plot No. 13, Ecotech-III, Greater Noida - 201306, U. P. India

Contents

1. Analyse Your Stress   8
2. The Stress Trigger   10
3. Assess Your Stress Levels   36
4. Stress and the Immune System   40
5. Stress Management   49
   Myths and Fact File   63

𝓛ife and stress are interwoven with each other. It depends on how you view life and how stress affects you. Stress has been defined as a non-specific response by the body to readjust. Some people readjust well physically and mentally with circumstances. Many of us, get upset or flustered over things. This affects your system, your day and your lifestyle.

It has been seen that those working in night shifts over a period of time are more prone to ulcers, high blood pressure and other diseases. Certain amount of stress is important to achieve targets but chronic stress often takes a heavy toll on a person. Chronic type of stress constantly keeps you under tension and makes you tired and ill. Take a stock of your life and its activities, now!

1 Analyse Your Stress

Are you under stress? Answer this questionnaire to find out.

1. Are you comfortable with your living surroundings?
   a. You are content with your home and its surroundings.
   b. You feel stressed out with the city pollution and its pace of life.
   c. You can manage with your pace of life and find home comfortable.
2. When it comes to your job, how would you place yourself?
   a. You are ambitious and motivated.
   b. You find work unsatisfactory and boring.
   c. You are satisfied with the job.

3. If you had a problem with a personal relationship
   a. You would pretend that there is no problem.
   b. You would get depressed.
   c. You would like to talk about it and get over with it.
4. How do you find life?
   a. You are in control of it.
   b. You are always looking for something you don't have.
   c. You are pleased by the way things are going.
5. While preparing to give a presentation or a lecture or speech in front of people…
   a. You are stimulated and thrilled.
   b. You panic.
   c. You are a little nervous but full of energy.

Stress is a highly individual phenomenon. It is strange in its own way – because when it occurs it becomes difficult for the body and mind to adjust to the pattern of life!

The more you answer (b) the more stressed out you are. Control your emotions during various situations; otherwise you can get into a sense of hopelessness or depression!

2 The Stress Trigger

Where does the stress arise from?

- It can arise from your innerself.
- It can be imbedded in you.
- It can also be hidden and cause a communication problem.
- It depends on how you function mentally and what you think, i.e., your attitude. E.g. a job transfer may be stressful for one person, but a great opportunity for the other !!

How does stress relate with you?

Worry?

Pain?

Discomfort?

Excitement?

Anxiety?

Fear?

Uncertainty?

Some Symptoms of Stress

Anxiety
Depression
Overeating
Negative thinking
Excessive sleeping
Diarrhoea
Constipation
Constant tiredness
Headache
Loss of appetite

Anger
Tension
Irritability
Itchy skin
Allergies
Smoking
Aching joints
Palpitations
Breathlessness

Women and Stress

The fluctuating estrogens in a woman's body can make her moody. During stress periods, estrogen levels drop in a woman. The adrenal glands produce more of stress hormones than estrogen. During this phase when estrogen drops, there can be a build up of arterial plaque increasing the risk of cardiac disease. By menopause the levels of estrogen in a woman drop by nearly 80%. This is an important turning point in a woman's life. Major changes from hot flushes to bone mass loss to osteoporosis can occur. Also, estrogen has a protective effect on the cardiovascular system till menopause. After menopause, women become susceptible to heart problems equivalent to that in men.

Men and Stress

Dropped levels of testosterone are both linked to physical and psychological stress. Testosterone is the hormone which gives men the masculine features of facial hair, deep voice and musculature.

Testosterone is linked to the dominant behaviour in men. It is also linked to the male perspective and their different traits compared to women. Their learning style, rationality and reluctance to express their feelings is completely male! Both sexes are different physically and mentally.

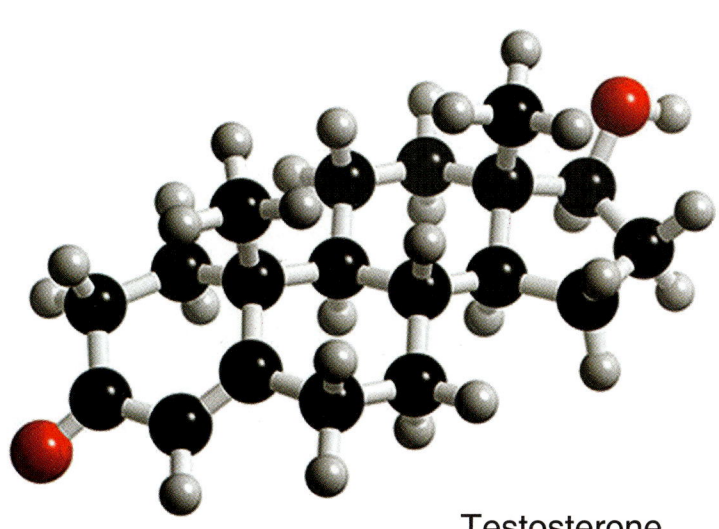

Testosterone

Hormones Linked to Stress

The Stress Hormone: Cortisol

Stress has become a part of our daily routine. Certain amount of stress is important for you to deal with life's ups and downs. When you experience stress of any kind, your body releases cortisol (a steroid hormone) into the blood stream. This stress hormone helps you cope with the day-to- day situations.

Cortisol is produced by your adrenal glands (a pair of small glands situated on the kidney). Your body is in a constant state of regeneration, breaking itself down, then rebuilding itself again. Cortisol is the important centre stage of this process. When you experience stress of any kind (excitement, anger, shock, surprise, fright) cortisol is released.

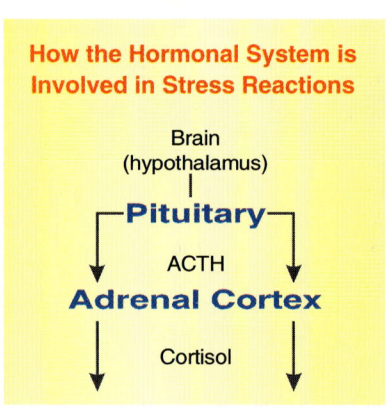

Cortisol influences the breakdown and utilisation of proteins, carbohydrates and fats in your diet. Excessive cortisol also carries out critical functions like helping maintaining your blood pressure and suppressing reactions like allergy, inflammation and pain.

Cortisol is produced more by your body in the morning than in the evening. It provides you with the energy to start your day. By evening your body's cortisol levels should fall by about 90%. Due to today's highly stressful life, many people produce more cortisol. Unlike men, elevated evening cortisol levels have been found in women who work outside their homes (especially those with small children).

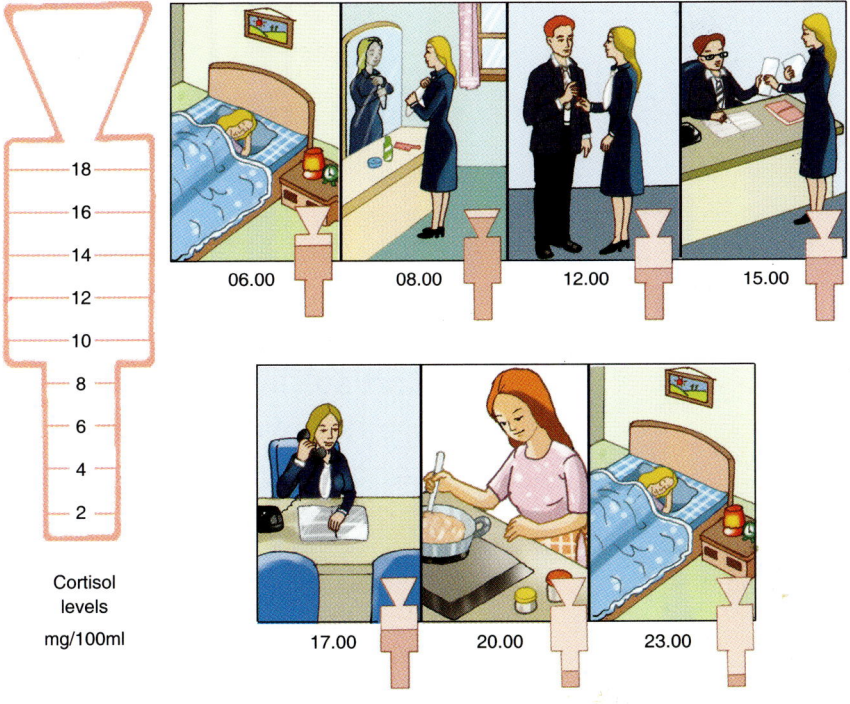

This is probably due to handling stress both at the work place and at home.

Chronically elevated cortisol levels are associated with health conditions like:

- Exhaustion
- High blood sugar
- Fat accumulation in the belly (abdominal region)
- Comprised immune function
- Bone loss
- Heart Disease
- Memory loss

Balancing Hormones

Serotonin, noradrenaline and dopamine are three important hormones produced by your body which help you feel "good and balanced" or in other words normal. The stress that you experience through various forms interferes with the production of these hormones.

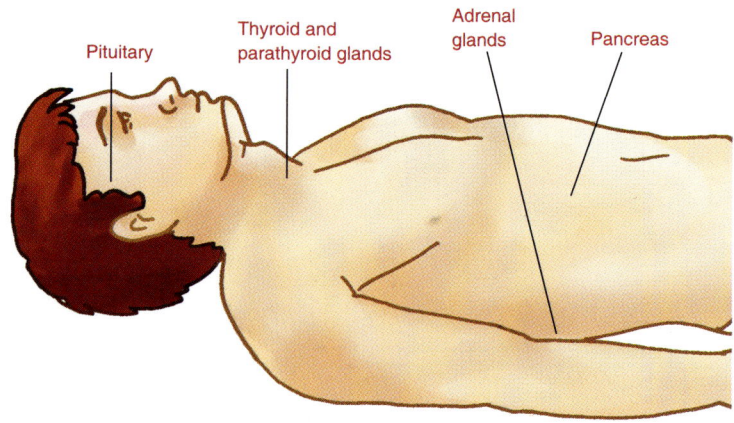

- Serotonin is a hormone responsible for a sound sleep. Stress can often disturb the production of this hormone, resulting in a disturbed sleep cycle.

    Serotonin is produced in the pineal gland inside the brain and helps control your body clock. Serotonin converts into melatonin (another hormone) and then again converts back into serotonin over a period of 24 hrs. This process helps in regulating your sleep cycle, body temperature and also regulates your energy.  The serotonin cycle synchronises with the cycle of the sun. It regulates itself according to the daylight and darkness. Therefore, some people in colder countries who are less exposed to the sunlight often experience seasonal depression during the long, dark winter months where serotonin production and regulation becomes irregular.

- Noradrenaline is produced by your adrenal glands. Noradrenaline is related to the adrenaline released by your body in times of stress. It gives you a burst of energy and is also linked with your daily energy cycle. Too much of stress drains you. It can deplete your energy, and deprive you of any motivation.

- **Dopamine** is a hormone which is linked to the pain killer hormone (endorphin, found in the brain). When stress is increased, your body compromises to produce dopamine and in turn it also compromises with your body's ability to produce endorphins. Your sensitivity to the sensation of pain increases. Dopamine also helps you experience the feeling of joy. If there is too much stress, too little dopamine is released. Due to less dopamine release, the feeling of joy is lost and you can feel depressed.

Stress therefore is both from inside and outside. There are regular chemical changes occurring due to various events and habits (attitude) occurring through body and mind.

It is all connected !

Stress can disrupt the production of serotonin, noradrenaline or dopamine, which in turn can affect the normal and healthy functioning of the body and result in depression.

Many antidepressants are especially designed to regulate the production of these three hormones and to help re-establish equilibrium of the body. If stress management techniques do not work for an individual he or she should consult a doctor.

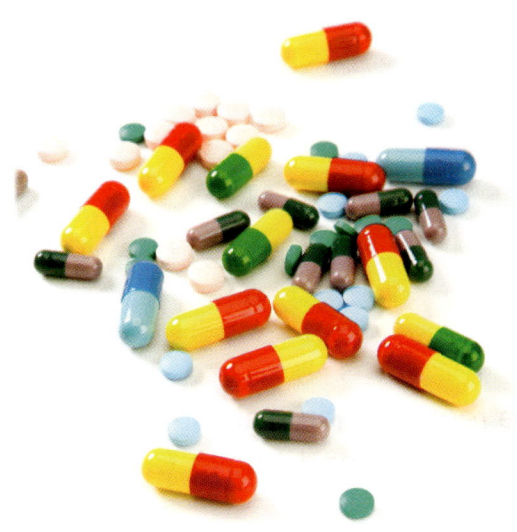

Effects of Stress

When your body experiences stress through direct or indirect physiological mechanisms it undergoes certain changes.

- An alarm message from the cerebral cortex of your brain is sent to the hypothalmus (another area of your brain). The hypothalmus then releases chemicals which trigger off the stress response.
- Your sympathetic system also gets stimulated with the chemicals. It prepares the body for any change or stressed situation.

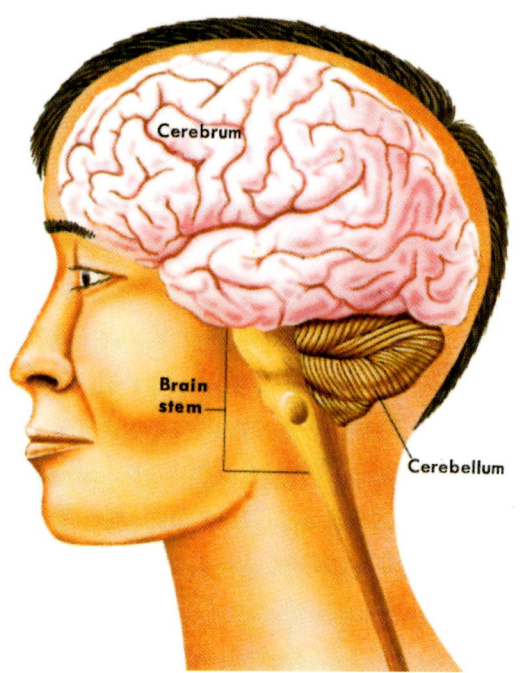

Tummy Trouble

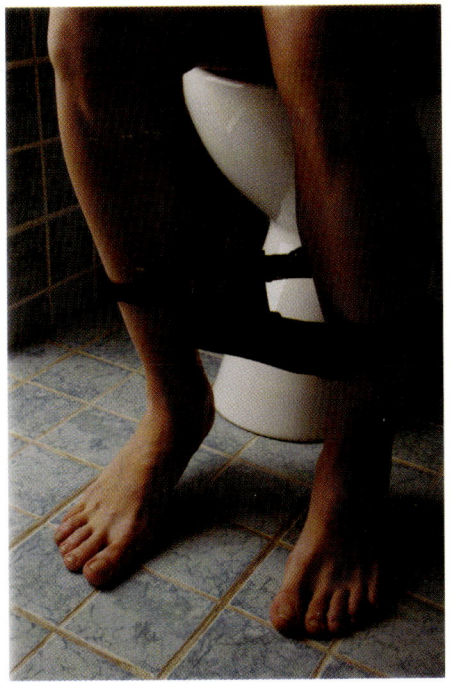

People with chronic stress or anxiety often experience nausea, vomiting, diarrhoea or stomach cramps. This is because when the body undergoes stress over a period of time the blood gets diverted from your digestive tract to the large muscles of your body. Stomach or intestines may empty their contents quickly, preparing the body for quick action. This chronic stress is often the cause of irritable bowel syndrome, colitis, ulcers and chronic diarrhoea.

Irritable Skin

Hormonal irregularities usually cause skin problems like acne. This can be aggravated by stress. Chronic or long-term stress besides causing chronic acne can contribute to other forms of dermatitis like psoriasis and lichen planus.

Pain

Migraines, arthritis and multiple sclerosis can worsen when a body is stressed out. An impaired immune system can worsen these diseases. Diseases like degenerative bone and joint involvement also get affected through stress. Stress management techniques often help the mind to deal with the pain.

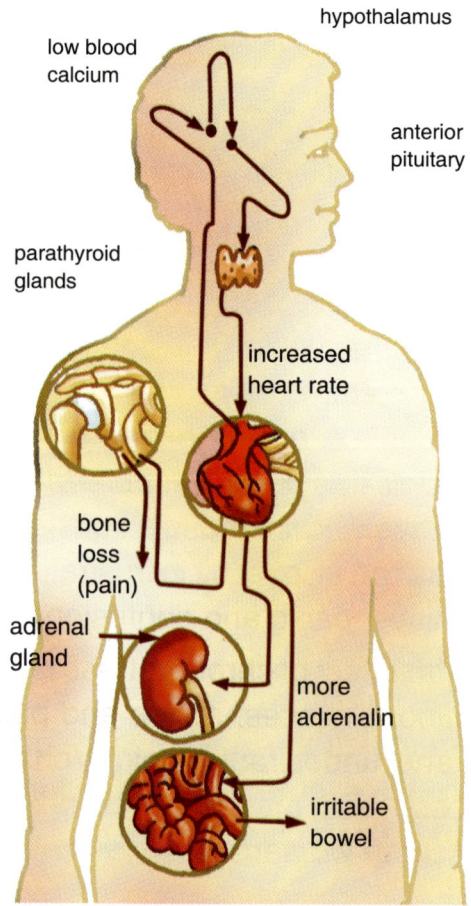

Cardiovascular System

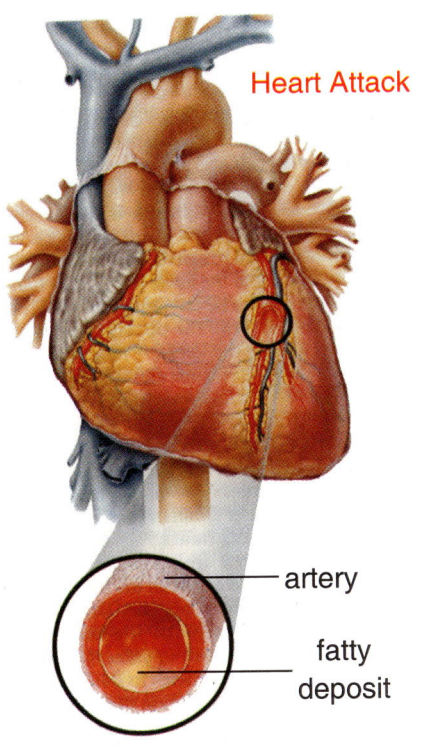

Heart Attack — artery, fatty deposit

Stress over a long period can lead to high blood pressure (hypertension). Stressed out people (who have long, irregular working hours) often get into an irregular lifestyle as well! Wrong eating habits (junk, fast food) with too much saturated fat, sweets, food low on fibre, have a direct effect on our health. To add to it, if you do not exercise but drink and smoke, then all this can contribute to the clogging of your arteries and increase your risk of a heart attack. Stress can also result in frustration, sweating, cold extremities, panic and confusion.

Long-term effect of chronic stress is depression, frequent minor illnesses, aches and pains, sexual problems and undesirable weight changes (both gain and loss). Also, medical conditions like asthma and arthritis can worsen.

Do not reach this stage as it sometimes is difficult to rectify completely the effects of long-term stress! Acute stress helps you deal with immediate situations. It helps you think clearly and respond fast. The immediate fight or flight situation is activated. Chronic stress on the other hand leads to malfunctioning of the brain. Forgetfulness and loss of concentration is the result.

Many people in their forties and fifties start forgetting and misplacing or losing things. This forgetfulness is actually linked to stress which is often at the peak of your life. This is due to work demand, growing up children, trying to achieve a successful personal career, and various other social and circumstantial demands. Don't let stress overburden the circuits of your mind.

How different parts of the body are affected by stress

Parts of Body	Reaction to Stress
Heart	Increased rate
Gut	Digestive process slows down
Pupils	Dilate, to help in vision
Lungs	Increased rate of respiration
Adrenal gland	Release more adrenaline
Skin	Increased sweating
Liver	More of glucose released, energy level increased

Negative Aspects of Stress

- Stress can damage body organs, the immune and the nervous system.
- Reaction of stress can result in the movement of fat from body fat stores and is used as fuel. This release of fat in turn can cause release of certain fat stored toxins resulting in an increase of free radicals.
- Stress can also deplete certain vitamins in your body.
- Your body can be weakened by stress as it affects your immune system making you susceptible to allergies and infections.
- It can also cause an increased heart rate, elevate cholesterol levels, and cause breathlessness and tense muscles.

Positive Aspects of Stress

Students facing an examination, high powered executives during presentations, doctors or paramedics during an emergency, sportsmen at championship games are all able to give a high performance due to this "power" stress. The problem is that while this stress is great in moderate amounts it becomes harmful in excess.

Life and stress are interwoven with each other.

Nature of Stress

- **Acute Stress:** It is interwoven with change. (It can be of good or bad type). Change that you are not used to (e.g. illness, divorce, change of job, marriage, etc.)

children *assets*

- **Periodic Stress:** Periodic stress happens for the period of a week or month or over a year – a car accident or breakdown, illness in the family, children not getting admissions in careers of their choice, sudden change in life, and so on.

- **Chronic Stress or Routine Stress:** It is day in and day out ! Starting from home hurriedly – always late at work place – stuck in a traffic jam – overworked – back home responsibilities, eating junk food – food not to your taste, not getting enough sleep – over and over again, throughout the week. All these can lead to stress. That's chronic stress for you. No change. No vacation. Its monotonous. Chronic stress catches up with you!. The body is tired. The brain refuses to think.

Types of Stress

Personal stress

It comes from events or circumstances in your personal life, e.g. examination, interviews, rift with a close friend or partner, etc.

Try and get your emotions under control. Some of the most effective techniques to manage personal stress are:

- Through friends
- Through head and body massage
- Exercise
- Through creative work
- Visualisation (e.g. of pleasant environment)

Social and environmental stress

Human beings are social creatures who live in a complex and interactive system i.e. society. In this system they have to abide by the norms laid down by the society.

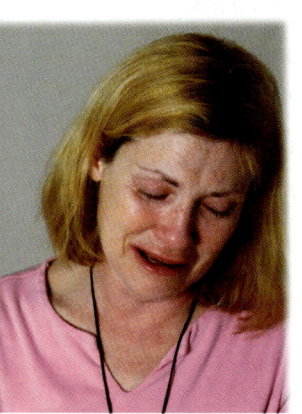

On the other hand environmental stress is dependent upon the world around you (e.g. If you live in a polluted area or in an area where you are allergic to the surroundings.) Changes in a household, addition or loss of a member or a pet in your life leads to both social and environmental stress.

Ways to help you through social and environmental stress are:

- Attitude adjustment
- Through creative thinking and putting it into practice.
- Discussing your problems with friends or close ones.
- Exercise
- Yoga and meditation

Physiological stress

Physiological stress is related to the response of the body during illness or pain. This type of stress is also related to hormonal changes in the body. In women, physiological stress stretches between premenstrual syndrome, pregnancy and menopause. Other disorders like chronic fatigue, insomnia, depression or eating disorders as well as certain other imbalances in the body can lead to physiological stress. Sometimes physiological stress can be beyond your control. A few ways to relieve and reduce it can be through:

- Proper nutrition
- Correct living habits
- Various types of massage (body, head, feet)
- Relaxation techniques (through music, reading, etc.)
- Herbal and vitamin supplementation
- Meditation

Psychological Stress

Almost all anxiety attacks and stress related mind-body illnesses are known to cause sleep disorders such as sleep apnoea, delayed sleep phase syndrome, and even oversleeping. In extreme cases stressors or causes of stress can even cause insomnia.

Chronic stress conditions can lead to various Attention-Deficiency Disorders such as ADD and ADHD, which are again products of the demands of modern life and its priorities.

Individuals with Attention-Deficiency Disorder, predominantly Inattentive Type (ADD) exhibit six or more symptoms of inattention and less than six symptoms of hyperactivity-impulsivity. They usually exhibit some of the following symptoms: inattention, distractibility, disorganisation, day-dreaming, lack of foresight, carelessness, forgetfulness, lack of motivation, lack of persistence, and procrastination.

Individuals with Attention-Deficiency Disorder, predominantly Hyperactive-Impulsive Type (ADHD) usually exhibit six or more symptoms of hyperactivity-impulsivity and less than six symptoms of inattention. They usually exhibit some of the following symptoms: hyperactivity, fidgeting, restlessness, excessive talking, inappropriate running and climbing often.

Causes of Stress

Sleeplessness

Overworking, socialising late till night, being on the net, watching late night movies or television are all stressors, especially if done on a daily basis. Sleep deprivation leads to irritability, confusion of the mind, lack of concentration and, eventually, ill health.

- Make enough time for sleep.
- Treat your sleep disorder.
- Avoid a suppressed immune system.
- Get enough exercise during the day.
- At night or evening your diet should contain more of tryptophan. Tryptophan is an amino acid that helps the body to produce serotonin, the chemical which induces sleep. Foods containing more of tryptophan are milk, yoghurt, rice, peanut butter, dates, figs and turkey.
- Eat a healthy, low fat, low carbohydrate dinner.

Caffeine and Caffeinated Products

- Do not drink (colas, coffee, etc are addiction) too many caffeinated drinks every day.
- Drinking two to three cups of coffee in a day supplies you with approximately 400 mg of caffeine. Caffeine releases adrenaline in your body which can exacerbate the effects of stress.

- Avoid dehydration

Our body is made up of 2/3 of water. Most people are mildly dehydrated – as they do not take in enough water. Unfortunately, they are not conscious of it. Mild dehydration (3-5% below body weight) goes unnoticed. It occurs while dieting, after exercise, vomiting, diarrhoea, etc. It can also occur after excessive consumption of alcohol and some illness.

Replenish yourself with 6-8 glasses of water every day. This detoxifies your body and helps in coping with stress.

Noise and the Media

Too much of the audio or visual media leads to a habit – called the "continuous noise habit". You need some kind of noise, (music, TV) in the background while you work or sleep. This subconsciously does not let you focus enough or give you a good pattern of sleep. Silence is not only therapeutic but energising. It helps you to live with yourself and at the same time destress you!

Worry

Are you a worrier? Do you find yourself worrying about things which are unlikely to occur? You cannot sleep over every small issue. Remember, worry has a negative effect on your body. It can lead to dry mouth, heart palpitations, panic and fatigue. Worry can become extremely stressful.

Alcohol

Alcohol should be taken in moderation – not more than 60 ml in a day and not necessarily every day. Avoid drinking late at night. Alcohol disrupts your pattern of sleep. It can cause snoring and sleep apnoea.

③ Assess Your Stress Levels

Assess the parameters given on the next page and add them up to know as to how much stress you are under.

Levels over 300 indicate that you are under heavy stress. Destress yourself or you may fall ill.

Event	Number Value
Death of a spouse	100
Divorce	073
Marital separation	065
Jail term	063
Death of a close family member	063
Personal injury or illness	053
Marriage	050
Fired from work	047
Marital reconciliation	045
Retirement	045
Change in family member's health	044
Pregnancy	040
Sex difficulties	039
Addition of family	039
Business readjustment	039
Change in financial status	038
Death of a close friend	037
Change in work	036
Change in number of marital disagreements	035
Mortgage payments or loan	031
Change in work responsibilities	029
Son or daughter leaving home	029
Trouble with in-laws	029
Outstanding personal achievement	028
Change in living conditions	025
Change in residence	020
Other changes	15-20
Vocation	013
Christmas season	012
Minor violation of the law	011

The Holmes-Rahe Social Readjustment Rating Scale

More stress produces more free radicals, which cause extensive damage to the body.

What are these Free Radicals?

Free Radicals

"Every day, each cell in the body generates tens of thousands of free radicals, by-products of normal metabolism. They tend to undermine neighbouring molecules. Pollutants augment the process. Antioxidants, which can neutralise free radicals, are among the body's mechanisms for stemming the damage".

Free radicals are a by-product of metabolism. Our body generates heat and energy and disposes off carbon dioxide. Free radicals are formed as a natural by-product of this process.

Food + oxygen = CO_2 + water + energy + free radicals

A single free radical can produce reactions involving thousands of damaged molecules along with new free radicals, before the process burns itself out or is reactivated.

Chain reactions of these radicals continue until antioxidants like Vitamin A, C, E, certain enzymes and minerals can quench this reaction.

It is only when there are too many factors forming free radicals and not enough antioxidants to quench these reactions that the "free radicals" start playing havoc with your health.

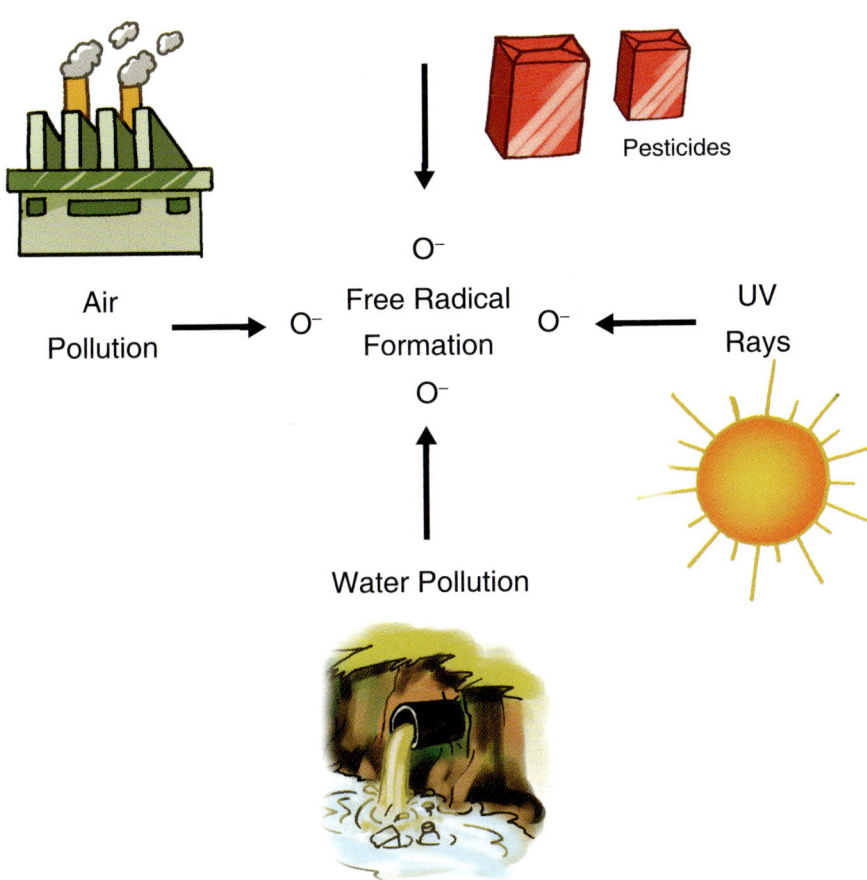

4 Stress and the Immune System

Steven Locke points out, "it is not stress itself which is immunosuppressive, but stress coupled with poor coping".

Stress and You

When we compromise on our self-esteem, we throw our body off balance. Due to the effects of physical and mental stress, low self-esteem, frustration, irritation and anger take over. Our spirit is destroyed. Bad bosses, domineering relationships can destroy you. Creativity and the joy of life is lost. The onset of diseases like schizophrenia, depression or suicidal tendencies is the result.

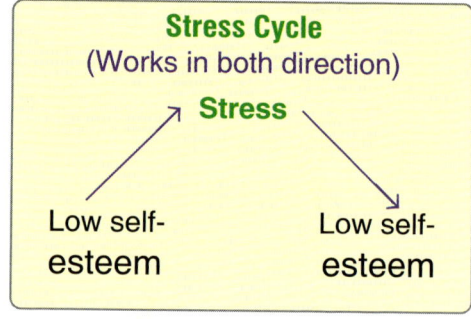

- Stress has been implicated in causing a deficient immune system. This is the body's defuse mechanism in dealing with stress. Mood swings also play a role in the effectiveness of the immune system.

- Inhibition of emotions result in stress, affecting health.
- Cardiovascular diseases are also known to be affected by stress.
- A positive attitude seems to help the immune system in fighting diseases. It is seen that people with positive emotions have a greater ability to fight off infectious diseases like the common cold.
- Social environment plays a significant role in the functioning of the immune system. A supportive social system (joint family) seems to increase the immunity of a person, helping in regulation of increased blood pressure and control of cardiovascular disease in a person.

- The brain itself possesses amazing healing powers. Normally, under optimal conditions the immune system helps the body to heal itself. The trouble begins when the body's equilibrium is disturbed or damaged due to long-term release of stress hormones. This results in an imbalance leading to inefficient working of the immune system.

So, keep stress within its limits. A lively spirit knows no bounds. A *bound* spirit has no life! Life is to live, so live to its best.

Stress Depletes Nutrients from the Body

The best thing is to target "your stress situation" with a nutrient attack.

Vitamin/ Mineral	Action	Found in
B1	Helps maintain nervous system. Helps in anaemia. May protect against heart disease.	Milk, whole grains, eggs, pork
B6	Boosts immune system. Relieves menopausal symptoms and relieves premenstrual syndrome. May protect against certain cancers.	Whole grains, cereals, milk, vegetables, fish meat
B12	Maintains nervous system. Helps in boosting memory. Increases growth and energy.	Milk, eggs, fish, liver, pork, beef
Zinc	Helps in boosting the immune system and healing.	Whole grains, eggs, meat, mushrooms
Iron	Boosts the immune system. Increases energy and prevents iron deficiency, anaemia	Wheat, bran, fruits like apple, dates
Selenium	Boosts immune system, keeps skin, hair and eyes healthy, improves liver.	Fish, bran, wheat green tomato, broccoli

Stress increases the need for zinc in the body. Zinc and Vitamin B6 are important for functioning of the thyroid gland which is a part of the immune system. Vitamin B6 also needs to be supplemented when stress of the body or mind increases.

Five Steps to Destress

We must find ways to destress ourselves. We need to control our stressful situations and destress our stress response.

Counselling

We all need to solve problems, often they are solved by friends and relatives. Sometimes we need professional help whatever be the kind, listen to it and then take your decisions.

Communicate with friends as that is a big "destressor" and boosts your immune system. Also think positively and stop inducing stress by focussing on negative thoughts. Before negative thoughts invade your mind, examine them and reject them. Try and relax your mind.

Channel Opening Therapies

T 'ai chi: This therapy is of Chinese origin and is based on "energy channel". The fundamental belief of T 'ai chi therapy is that "energy channels" flow around the body. If the channels are not kept clear the 'chi', or intrinsic energy of the body gets affected. This energy cannot flow properly and the individual concerned suffers.

T 'ai chi is performed as a series of controlled precise movements, thereby calming the brain and leading to greater control over emotions.

Acupuncture: It is also a Chinese remedy practised by therapists. This practice consists of a technique which releases the flow of 'chi' by placing special needles along special routes in the body. Keeping the channels open through this practice helps remedy many health problems, including stress.

Shaitsu: It means "finger pressure" and is a Japanese therapy. It helps unlock energy channels. The therapist practising shiatsu, identifies the energy channel and determines which needs unlocking and puts pressure on specific points to unlock the channels, making the *chi* flow freely.

Pets and Children

Pets relieve stress. By spending sometime with them they can make you feel good. If you have young children at home, take them to the park. Play with them. You will forget what bothered you during the day.

Osteopathy

In cases of trauma or injury, not only do physical problems come up, but stress is also involved. Backache, which is a common complaint, is often caused by muscle tension, due to misalignment of the vertebrae. This discomfort brings about stress. These problems can be corrected by osteopathy. The osteopathic process involves massage, which itself is stress relieving.

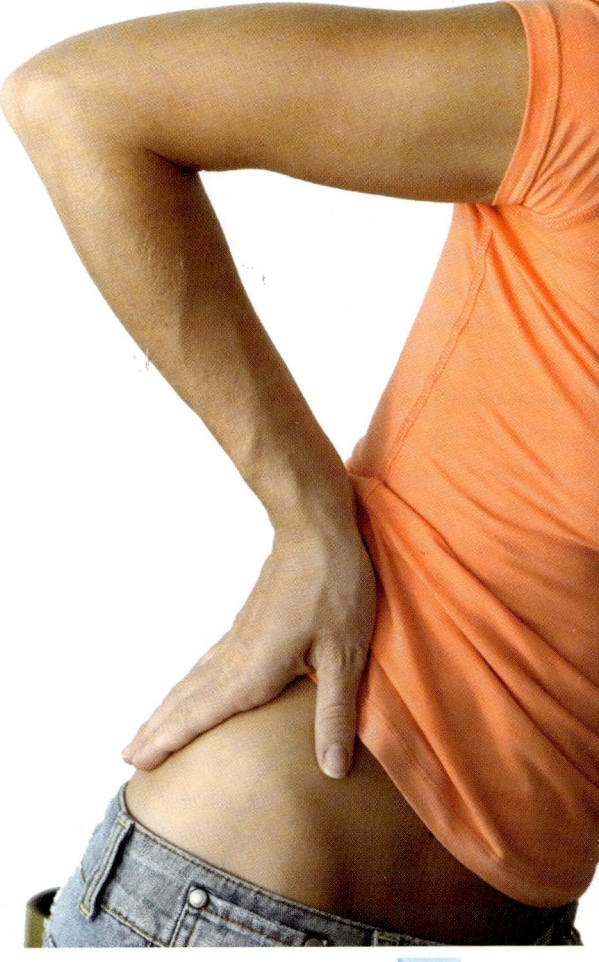

Visualisation

Visualisation involves using your imagination for visual imagery. It can be done with your eyes shut. When you feel stressed or tense visualise yourself in a pleasant surrounding like on a beach with palm trees, the blue sky and ocean or near the mountains, etc. Get over your "worried" self and try and relax with this powerful technique of visualisation, you will feel calm and happy.

5 — Stress Management

The most important part of stress management is time technique.

Each day

- Get organised
- Give life a direction

Get organised

- Understand your priorities.
- Don't run around aimlessly.
- List your priorities for the day.
- Work out a realistic time for the job alloted. From that time frame derive your time table for the day. Don't forget to include travelling time!
- Cross out every morning what has been done previously and chalk out your new list. If some things have cropped up unexpectedly, like an unscheduled meeting, car break down or an emergency at home deal, with it calmly. A few minutes may upset your schedule timewise, but do not let it upset your mood and day.

- Delegate work which can be done by others (your secretary, staff, etc).

    Check with them after a period of time or insist on feed back. Don't get into a hassle, by checking on them every few minutes.

As you finish each job, reward yourself with a break – a glass of water, a couple of minutes of relaxation exercise or breaks of fresh air.

Give Life a Direction

Control your ambitions

Take control of your emotions and life's little problems will take care of themselves. Reduce your anxieties and do not let stress get to you.

Manage time sensibly and keep a positive and cheerful outlook.

Balance your diet

A well balanced diet and nutritional supplementation can help counter the increased demands made by your body when under stress.

Start incorporating destress and management techniques in your daily routine.

See how good you start feeling at the end of the day!

Exercise: The stress buster

Various forms of exercises can be done, from bicycling to joining a gym.

Exercise helps you physically get your mind off your problems and burn off the "stress hormones"

Weight lifting

It is an important part of an adult's fitness routine. At about 35 years of age you start losing bone mass. The susceptibility towards fractures increases. Weight lifting helps in counteracting bone loss.

Weight lifting also builds bone mass, helps in preventing osteoporosis and increases muscle tone. Your body also burns more calories because the more muscles you have, the more calories you burn during your aerobic workout.

Stronger bones and muscles are a boon for working through middle and older age.

Yoga and Meditation

Yoga increases oxygen and respiratory levels, which in turn help in circulation and digestion. Release of toxins through perspiration occurs and creates an unreceptive environment for virus to act on the body.

Yoga helps mind and body to relax. It modifies heart rate and high blood pressure. This in turn can reduce anxiety and stress. Yoga also helps in increasing energy levels.

Meditation is a mental exercise. It calms the mind and increases its concentration.

Music Therapy

Music helps you unwind. You should listen to bhakti or devotional music in the morning and light music in the evening.

Hydro Therapy

Water is the essence of life. Have a light shower before going to bed or at least wash your face and feet with water which is neither too hot nor too cold (depending upon the weather). It helps the body to relax and gives sound sleep. Proper sleep is extremely important for an active and energetic mind.

Massage

- Massage helps activate muscle and skin.
- It also improves circulation and organ function.

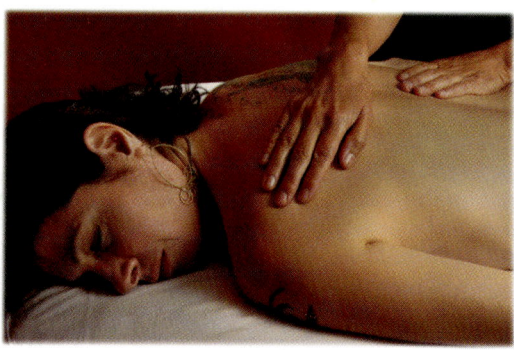

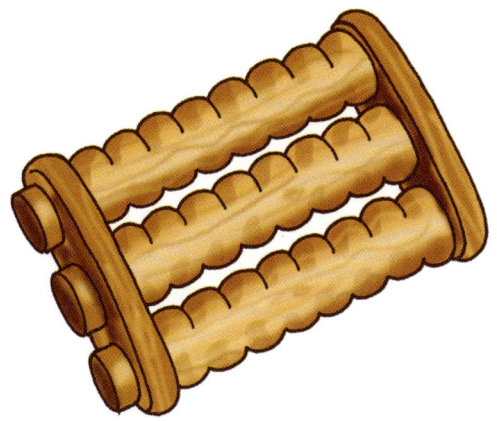

- Massage helps destress as it aids in healing body and mind.
- With a regular massage, the joints become more flexible and the posture also improves.
- A massage therapist helps relieve stress as he is trained to knead and manipulate muscles and tissues in the body.

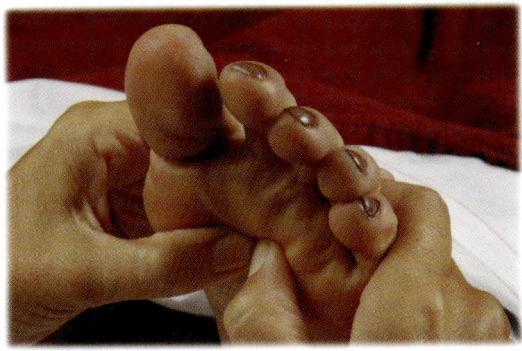

Relaxation Techniques

Set aside a few minutes for yourself. Go to a quiet room or an area in the house where you can do what you really want to do like

- Making a call
- Read the paper or magazine
- Drink or eat something peacefully.
- Take a few minutes off from the daily routine of home, office and life! Do what pleases you. It's a stress buster !! Give your thoughts a break! An overworked brain finds it difficult to function.

Doodle ! Relax ! Unwind !

You will find yourself coming up with a logical solution.

- Listen to some music, massage yourself or even have a bath or shower. Relax for a few minutes.

- Herbalism and aromatherapy would help destress.

Herbal Therapy

It is an ancient therapy. Some of the best known "allopathic drugs" used today have their origin in herbs. Unfortunately, a lot of their preparations in the correct proportions were not passed on to the younger generations. Aspirin as we know is synthesised from willow bark and digitalis comes from foxgloves. There are other innumerable herbs.

Some of the known relaxing herbs are:

Evening primrose oil: For premenstrual tension, for high cholesterol and arthritis (both known to be stress related).

Lavender: Relaxes you, calms your body and helps you sleep well.

Herbal Teas

Certain herbal teas help destress and aid digestion.

Aroma Therapy

Natural and aromatic plants are used to enhance physical, emotional and spiritual well-being. Smell is also known to be therapeutic.

Using scents in a daily routine can improve your confidence. Aromatherapy helps in stimulating the production of endorphins in the body. It also helps enhance the immune system and can correct the imbalance in the body.

Some Beneficial Oils

Oil	Beneficial Effect
Sandalwood	Helps in reflection
Jasmine	Euphoria
Pine	Relieves fatigue
Rose	Brightens communication
Basil	Alertness increases
Lemon	Refreshing
Peppermint	Digestive aid
Eucalyptus	Refreshing
Lavender	Helps in relaxation

Behavioural pattern to stress

Do you belong to the Type A or Type B personality?

If you are temperamentally aggressive, competitive, always in a hurry, you belong to Type A.

If you are cool and calm in nature, you work at things patiently, one thing at a time, you then belong to Type B personality.

Remember Type A people need to slow down and work coolly as their stress levels are high and they are the ones who are prone to heart attacks.

Managing Stress

Are you constantly muddled? Is time heavy on your hands? Are you constantly late or behind schedule at work?

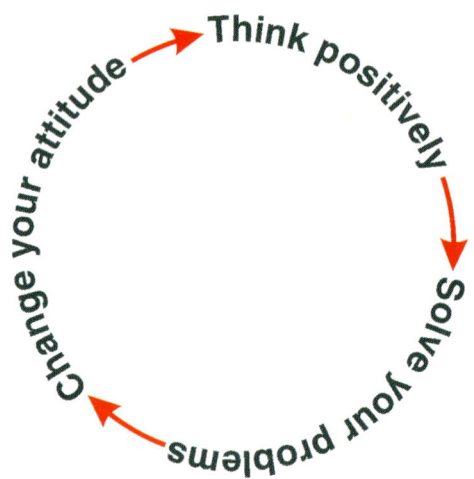

After a long day at work

- You can dip you feet in warm water. Massage your feet.
- Pranayaam or deep breathing exercises are good as a daily practice.
- Meditation helps you focus better. Think of pleasant things. It helps you feel good.
- Soft music, flowers, a green patch, playing with children and animals, helps you relax.
- A good brisk walk in the open is an excellent relaxation technique.

Give yourself a little time after a long day.

- *Destress your body and mind daily.*

Last but not the least, have nutritious food. Food should be taken at regular intervals. Correct food timing with enough vegetables, fruits, medium amounts of carbohydrates and protein are important. Drink at least 6-8 glasses of water to clean and detoxify your system. In this fast-paced world today, learn how to destress early in life or age will fast catch up with you!

Myths and Fact File

Myth

Yoga classes will tire me out more.

Fact

Yoga will help you tone up your muscles. At the same time, meditation will help you relax and destress.

Myth

I need lot of ghee, oils and sweets in my diet to give me the strength to work the whole day.

Fact

The above are all fattening. Fruits give you slow releasing sugar to help your mind work. Vegetables provide fibre, minerals and co-enzymes for a healthy body and mind. Roti or whole wheat bread provides you with energy. Too much oil and sweets are deterimental to health.